Lux Frenchies Vol 1.

Written by Whitney Swopes Emmons
Illustrated by Lynne Lillge

Copyright © 2023 by Whitney Swopes Emmons, Chelsey Lynne Lillge, and
Italic Stories (a division of Mythic North Press, LLC)

All rights reserved, including the right to reproduce this book or portions thereof in any form.

https://www.italicillustratorshop.com/
https://www.mythicnorthpress.com/

ISBN: 978-1-954177-40-6

This book is dedicated to my children, Mattie and Kohen, and all dog lovers around the world.

Love always,

Momma Lux

Whitney Emmons

I also have my mom, Velveeta and dad, Versace.

Their Lux adventures will be theirs to tell.

They are great.
I love them.
The best part is my dog family is close by.

Meet Chelsey, my mom. She is an artist. She is loving, kind, and a free spirit; much like me.

Meet Mark.
He is my dad.
For work, he is an inspector for many things in the industrial construction field. His job keeps him on the road.
We are going to have lots of adventures going around the United States for work.

Meet my girl Aleya. She is the most amazing girl there is. She loves me unconditionally and is always down to share snacks, cuddle, and play.
She and I are connected at the hip.
We are bonded for life.

Meet my little buddy Easton.
He is a baby, like me. He is gentle.
We are cuddle buddies, we like to
watch cartoons, and he might sneak me
a few of his snacks.

My life is wonderful.
My family is full of love, trust, and are all around the coolest people I know.

I can't wait to see where all the adventures take us.
Could we go to Oklahoma the plains state?

Wherever we go and what ever we see,
there is one thing I know;
the love of my family is pure, whole, and quiet frankly a LUX kind of love in all ways possible.

Aleya, Easton I am so glad to be your dog brother. I will always protect you, lick your tears, make you giggle, cuddle when your sick, cuddle when your blue.

www.ingramcontent.com/pod-product-compliance
Lightning Source LLC
Chambersburg PA
CBHW060411010526
44107CB00006B/647